I0504316

CAREER HACKS

65 Ways to

Become a Workplace Superstar
Create a Satisfying Work Life
Find a Meaningful Career
and
Overcome Obstacles to Your Success

Other Books by Ron Engeldinger

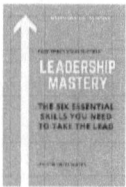

Leadership Mastery: Six Essential Skills You
Need To Take The Lead

Your Plan for Success: A Step by Step Guide to Help You Set Goals and Live the
Life You Are Meant to Live

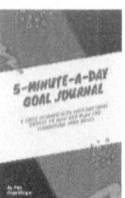

5-Minute-a-Day Goal Journal: A daily planner with inspirational quotes to help
you plan and accomplish your goals

Make it a Great Day Gratitude Journal: Cultivate a habit of gratitude. bringing joy,
inspiration, and reflection into your life

CONTENTS

INTRODUCTION

In the world today, getting ahead and making the most out of the career path you are on is harder than ever. Competition in the workplace is fierce, and the world is rapidly changing. Do you know what it takes to become successful in your endeavors? Do you know how to confidently take control of your future? Do you want to stand out as a superstar in your field? Or, do you want to transition into a completely new career?

Here is a book that gives you the resources that you need for growth and success in your work life. This book has been designed to give you the advice you need to move forward, whether you want to improve your current situation or you want to move on to something else. This book will answer your questions in a straightforward manner and an easy to read style. The tips offered in this book will enable you to confidently move forward toward the life you are meant to live.

With many years of experience as an effective leader and an academic career studying what makes people successful, I have discovered what it takes to get ahead in any organization. I learned that a well-crafted plan and an organized approach sets individuals up for achieving their dreams. As a teacher and consultant, both in the U.S. and abroad, I have nurtured thousands of students of all ages as they became successful in their professional endeavors.

I offer the insights that I gained through my own success as I moved up the career ladder and through my experiences as I developed the future leaders in my organization. My goal is to share what I have learned so that you will be prepared to meet the challenges and guide yourself on the road to success.

Many people have taken control of their lives and began achieving their goals by following the process found in this helpful guide. Whether you are just beginning your life's journey, you feel stuck in your current situation or feel you are meant for greater things, the tools that I offer will lead you on a path to success. If you know that you want more out of life but aren't sure what you want, this book will help you clarify your current situation, and it will help you discover how to go about creating the future you deserve.

The tips I share with you have provided me with opportunities for success in my career and in my life. I progressed from an inexperienced employee to managerial positions. I ultimately achieved positions of authority and was responsible for overseeing hundreds of employees. I guided the development of my employees and set them up on their own path to success.

CHAPTER ONE – BECOME A WORKPLACE SUPERSTAR

Over the course of more than thirty years spent supervising people and being supervised by others, I have gained considerable insight into how individuals can be successful in the workplace. I have had many successes and I also made many mistakes as part of my learning experience. During my career I had a long history of advancement, and I was promoted to the highest levels in more than one organization. Along the way, I also experienced being fired, being downsized, quitting bad jobs, changing companies and moving into completely new career paths. The knowledge I gained through the variety of workplace experiences helped me learn how some people become superstars at work, while others continually struggle.

My first full-time job after college was a manager-trainee position at a local pizza restaurant. I didn't have any restaurant or management experience, and my college degree was in geology. I think I was hired because I did okay with the job interview, and the manager did not have many other applicants. When I reported to the job on the first day, I found out that another manager trainee had also been hired.

I soon realized that there was only one position available, and the manager's secret plan was to pit the two of us against each other to see which one was the best. That was my first on-the-job learning experience. Eventually, I learned how to earn the respect of my co-workers, the trust of the people who reported to me and the support of my supervisors.

Two years later, I not only remained with the company but I had been promoted to become the general manager of another restaurant in the organization. I never heard what happened to the other trainee but I know he only lasted a few months.

Why was I successful and the other person not? I think it is because I became a student of the workplace. I committed myself to becoming a success by observing, by learning what worked and what didn't work, and by applying the knowledge that I gained. The top management of the organization came to realize that.

My father used to tell me, "do your job well and you will get noticed, that's all you need to do to get ahead in the workplace." That may have worked for him several decades ago, but I found out that is only part of the formula for success. You have to do more than simply performing your job duties to get noticed and move ahead in any workplace. You need to become a workplace superstar to gain the recognition and success that you deserve.

In every workplace that I encountered, I began to look at how others in the organization were standing out and advancing in their careers, and I started to emulate what they were doing. I also paid attention to the people who struggled, so I could avoid their mistakes. I realized that some simple changes in my attitude and behavior made a huge difference, I began to move forward in my career, and I learned what it takes to be successful in the workplace. Here are some of the actions that carried me forward.

Be a problem-solver instead of one who simply reports problems

No matter what industry you are in, there are always problems to solve. When you have to go to your supervisor with a problem, go prepared with a potential solution at the same time. As a supervisor, one of the most frustrating situations I found myself in was when an employee came to me saying, "We've got a problem," and then expecting me to provide the solution on the spot. The employees that I valued most were those who came to me and said, "We have a problem and here is how I think we may be able to solve it."

By conveying a potential solution when you present a problem, you open up a dialogue. The solution you offer may not be the one finally implemented but, even in that case, you are making a positive contribution to the conversation. It is possible that your supervisor has a different solution in mind and may want to go on a different path. It is also possible that the solution that you present is one that the supervisor has not thought of. Bringing a suggestion shows that you are a team player who takes initiative. The key is that you want to be able to show your willingness to give the problem some thought rather than expecting your supervisor to come up with all the answers.

Keep abreast of industry trends

No matter what business you are in, the state of the industry is constantly evolving. The use of technology has not only become commonplace, it has become necessary for every field. Today, even jobs that were once performed by manual labor are increasingly relying on machines. Whether it is using robotics to assemble automobiles, planting rows of corn by use of GPS tracking systems, or selling shoes using technology to determine an exact fit, the job cannot be done well today without utilizing technology. In every industry, effectivity and efficiency are continually improving.

The repair shop where I have my cars serviced has undergone a massive evolution over the several decades that I have been entrusting my car care to them. To be able to repair vehicles as the automotive technology has evolved, they have had to continually keep abreast of what new products and techniques are required to perform their job. That trend is occurring in all industries. For example, sophisticated forecasting software is now indispensable to sales and marketing personnel. Whatever your occupation is, and whatever your industry is, new tools and processes are continually being developed.

You will become a workplace superstar by learning everything you can about the new trends in your job, your company, and your industry. The internet can be a valuable tool for keeping abreast of the industry. Read news articles about your field, check out what your competitors are doing, and read company reports. Join an industry association and take advantage of your membership to attend local meetings. Read any newsletters, case studies, or informative articles that the association publishes.

Carry and use a notebook or the note-taking function on your phone

I have always felt that I had a good memory. However, I learned early in my career that I could not always remember the details of conversations as well as I wanted to. So, I developed the habit of carrying a notebook around whenever I met with others in the organization. I would take notes about conversations, and I would record my thoughts about any situation I was faced with. Occasionally, I didn't have a notebook with me, for example when I had a chance encounter with someone that led to an important conversation. In those cases, I would write down my thoughts as soon as I was back at my work station.

I learned that it is important to document everything. When you are given an assignment, write it down. When you give someone an assignment, write it down. Listen closely to the conversation and then write down what you hear and also write down what your views are about the topic of the conversation. At times, I felt it necessary to focus intently on the conversation rather than making notes. In those instances, I wrote down my recollection of the conversation and my thoughts about it as soon afterword as I could.

I also used my notebook to record my observations. As a school administrator, I would make it a point to take the time to drop in on classrooms. When I noticed something the instructor was doing or saying that impressed me, I made notes so that I could pass along the idea to other instructors. I would also use the notebook as a personal brainstorming aid. When a thought about any topic came to mind, I would write it down. Later when I looked at these random thoughts, I could more thoroughly develop ideas for solving problem, making decisions, or improving performance.

Be appropriately pushy

Be assertive but not aggressive is the motto I have lived by in my various work situations, both as an employee and as a manager. It is important to remember that if you don't speak up, you don't have a voice in what occurs. As an employee, I learned that I must stand up for myself and my ideas. When I was given an assignment, I asked my supervisor how often a progress report was expected, and I made sure to submit them in a timely manner. When I had a noteworthy accomplishment, I made sure that my supervisor was aware of it.

My philosophy was that if my supervisors felt I was being too pushy, they would tell me. I never had a supervisor tell me that I was giving them too much information. However, I have had supervisors tell me they appreciated me keeping them informed. The one caution I will make is to make sure you are not wasting your supervisor's time. Asking questions that have already been answered or constantly producing reports that do not add any new information may backfire, and you will be seen as too pushy.

As a supervisor, I learned that I could not assume that my instructions would always be carried out when I gave them to the people who reported to me. There could many reasons for their failure to take action. Maybe they didn't understand what I wanted them to do, maybe they didn't have the resources, or maybe they didn't share my urgency. I had to follow up to make sure they understood what was required, and if the instructions had been carried out. However, I learned that how I approach this follow up was important.

Communicate – make sure you understand and are understood

Speak clearly and confidently. Get to the point. Provide background information if necessary but carefully consider how much is necessary. A well-thought-out, concise message will communicate your message much more effectively than a long, rambling speech. Avoid jargon and acronyms unless you are sure the listener understands the terms.

Listening is also an important aspect of communication. Pay attention to the person speaking. Paying attention means that you make eye contact and avoid possible distractions. The other person must recognize that you are genuinely interested in what she or he has to say. Practice the art of active listening by focusing on the conversation and responding appropriately to what the other person is saying.

Check to make sure you understand what is said and that your message is understood. Repeat back, in your own words, to the other person what you heard them say. Ask them to paraphrase or summarize what you said. This will let you know if you are both on the same page.

Follow instructions

When your supervisor directs you to do a particular task, do it. It may seem to be common sense, but many people run into difficulty on the job because they don't follow instructions. Certainly, if you don't have the knowledge or skill to complete the task, make sure to let your supervisor know about your reservations before you take it on. However, if it is something you can do but don't want to do, the best course of action is to do it. As a supervisor, it was frustrating when employees failed to follow my instructions.

If what you are directed to do is time consuming, and you think it will take you away from other important duties, you may be able to negotiate the scope of the project or the deadline to make it more manageable. When you are unclear why you have been asked to do that particular task, ask your supervisor for clarification. Certainly, if you feel that what you are asked to do is unethical or illegal, be open with your supervisor and explain why you don't want to follow the instructions. Otherwise, avoid the temptation to procrastinate, stall, or do an incomplete job. Workplace superstars take on the assignments they are given and complete the tasks to the best of their ability.

Think transferability of ideas

When writing a letter of recommendation for me, a former supervisor wrote that one of my talents was that I could take a creative approach to problem solving. He explained that, when faced with an obstacle, I would take actions that had worked in a different setting and apply them to the current circumstance.

For example, I was able to apply the concepts I learned about customer service in the restaurant industry when I directed the student services function at a small college. I decided to treat each student as if he was a customer at my restaurant. After all, the students really were our customers, even though many people in higher education do not recognize that fact. Applying the customer service attitudes and techniques I had learned in restaurants, I was able to better connect with the students and to meet their needs.

Can something that works in another situation or industry apply to yours? Approaching challenges or problems often requires a new way of looking at the problem or challenge. Find creative solutions by looking beyond the immediate problem. What have you have done in different situations that may be an approach to take in this situation?

Seek cooperation even in difficult situations

In even the best functioning workplace situations, conflicts sometimes arise. You may think one solution to a problem is the best approach, while someone else may have a solution that he or she feels is better. Personality clashes, a high-stress environment, scarce resources, misinformation and poor communication can all lead to situations where the tension between co-workers reduces the efficiency and effectiveness of the organization.

When you are involved in circumstances such as this, you must look for ways to make the situation less difficult. Approach the situation with a positive attitude. Remind yourself that the other person may have valid reasons for their position and seek to find common ground between your position and theirs. You may be able to develop a hybrid solution to the problem where you incorporate portions of each person's suggestions to develop a plan.

Tensions can often be diffused when you signal to the other person that you are willing to cooperate, and that you want to listen to and understand what they are saying. A high-functioning organization can be identified by the cooperation and collaboration that is displayed at all levels of the workplace. No matter what their job function is, or how high they are in the hierarchy of the organization, workplace superstars shine by seeking to establish a cooperative environment in their work setting.

Do it now if it takes less than five or ten minutes

When you have a task that you can do quickly, it is generally best to do it right away. Don't succumb to the temptation to put it off. Procrastination can rear its head anytime but, for me, it seems to be especially present when it is a simple task. When I am faced with these simple, easy-to-do tasks, I have the tendency to tell myself, "I can do this anytime, so I will take care of it later."

When I put it off with the belief that I would do it later, it was easily forgotten. For example, when I finally did get around to responding to an email, it was often too late, and I missed the chance to add my thoughts. If you are like me, that simple task nags at you in the back of your mind. I find myself uneasy when I think about not having done it already. Just do it and move on.

Whether it is writing a note to a colleague or responding quickly to an email question, I found that it was best to get it done immediately. Others will appreciate it when you respond quickly or take care of the little tasks right away.

Manage electronic intrusions, create blackout periods

Today, more than ever, we are constantly bombarded with interruptions. The world has almost immediate access to us through our electronic devises. I work at my computer throughout the day so, even when I have my phone turned off I have the urge to regularly check my email or look at news sites to see what is happening in the world. Electronic intrusion can be a disrupter that diverts our focus and reduces our effectiveness.

I realized that I was logging onto email several times an hour and, because of that, my productivity was suffering. So, I made the decision to limit the number of times I looked at email. For me, checking every two hours was appropriate to keep current with information while maintaining a focus on my work tasks. I let everyone in my organization know that I would check emails at specific times. Decide how often you really need to check in and put it on your daily schedule. If someone needed an immediate response from me, they could give me a phone call.

Pay attention to non-verbal communication

While effective verbal interaction with your supervisor and coworkers is essential, strong communicators also understand that non-verbal cues are equally important. Positive non-verbal signs include maintaining eye contact, displaying an attentive posture (such as slightly leaning forward), and responding with appropriate facial expressions (such as smiling during a light moment or showing sympathy when the situation calls for it). Negative non-verbal signs include actions that give off the appearance of being distracted or disinterested. Actions such as looking at the clock, fidgeting, or doodling while someone is speaking to you are distracting non-verbal cues that indicate indifference and a lack of respect.

Pay attention to the non-verbal actions of others when you are speaking to them. Do they seem to be focused on what you are saying? Are they maintaining eye contact? If you sense that they are distracted, you may need to change your approach to the conversation so that you are getting your message across. If you come across as boring or judgmental, your message may be lost. Ask direct questions and observe their behavior in response to what you are saying. You may want to ask them directly about what you are observing.

Think about how you act when you are listening to someone. What non-verbal cues are you demonstrating? Are you intently listening or are you thinking about something besides the conversation? We don't always recognize our non-verbal behaviors, so it is a good idea to ask someone you trust to provide feedback. What actions are you taking when they are talking to you? Do they feel you are listening to what you are saying? Actively listening with intention is a skill that you can nurture.

Think about fitness, even short walks

Several years ago, I began walking to improve my health. I was determined to walk at least forty-five minutes a day but, with a full time job I wasn't sure where I would find the time. When I looked at how I was spending my time, I realized that I watched television for more than an hour every night. When I thought about it, I decided that walking to improve my health was more important to me than watching television, and I began an evening walking program.

Developing a fitness routine has many benefits. In addition to the health benefits, being physically active helps you clear your mind and maintain focus. It can increase stamina and create a positive mental state that makes you more productive. Find a regular exercise time that fits your schedule and develop an appropriate exercise routine to fit your body's needs. For me, a daily aerobic walk every evening set me up for the next day. When I wasn't able to walk, I noticed that I was less engaged in my work and more easily fatigued the following day.

If your job function allows it, I recommend taking a break when you can to get away from your work station and walk around. Even short walks during work breaks help renew your energy and allow you to be more productive. Whenever I could I would go outside and walk around during my lunch break. I found that this gave me a physical and mental boost that carried through the afternoon.

Improve your presentation skills

One of my first work supervisors suggested that I take a workshop on public speaking. My job at that time was directing a small workgroup of about twenty employees. I didn't feel uncomfortable talking to that small group, but I had never been required to speak to a larger audience. My supervisor told me he believed that public speaking was a valuable skill and one that I should become comfortable doing.

I was amazed at how much I learned from the workshop. The class exercises taught me how to prepare for talking to a large audience and provide information in an engaging manner. I learned the mechanics of speech, and I gained a confidence that stayed with me throughout my career. In later years, I was regularly called upon to speak to groups of all sizes. I felt at ease in every speaking assignment, even when the audience numbered in the hundreds or thousands.

Many people feel uneasy when they are asked to talk to a group. In my experience, the fear of public speaking haunts a large segment of the population. If you are unsure about your confidence or ability, a workshop or support group will definitely be worth it.

Take your communication skills to another level with an improvisation or story telling workshop

If do not feel comfortable with your public speaking skills, you may want to consider a class on improvisation or learn more about story telling. Often these classes or workshops are offered by local theater groups, and they are elective classes at many community colleges and universities. In an improvisation class, you will improve your ability to think on your feet and respond to the other person's message.

Improvisation classes also help you sharpen your listening skills. Taking part in an improvisation exercise requires that you focus completely on what the situation is and what the others are saying. You are required to respond to what the other person says or does, and your words and actions should carry the story forward.

Proficiency in story telling will be valuable in any business situation. It helps with forming connections with others in the workplace and is especially valuable when you need to explain complex theories or processes. In a story telling class, you will learn how to craft stories that are meaningful without being tedious. The best bosses I have had through the years were always good story tellers.

Put letters after your name with a college degree or professional accreditation

I am a strong proponent of life-long learning. Throughout my career I have continually sought out opportunities to learn more about whatever I was engaged in. Whether it is a two-year Associate Degree at a community college or a higher degree at a university or college, there are abundant options. I firmly believe that whatever route you take in a higher education setting, applying your enhanced knowledge will take you a long way to becoming a workplace superstar. In addition, many studies have demonstrated that attaining a college degree increases your income potential.

Another way to add letters after your name is to earn an industry certification. Many fields, from a hair dresser to a stock broker, have professional organizations. By joining a professional organization in your industry, you will meet others in the field and learn about the latest trends. In addition, many professional organizations offer classes or workshops that can lead to a professional accreditation. Not only will you learn more about the ins and outs of your profession, you will also receive a diploma or certificate attesting to your increased knowledge.

Increase your productivity with a time journal

Over the years, I realized that I was often not using my time as efficiently as I could be. I eventually learned strategies that helped me capture the time that I needed to juggle everything in my life, and one of the simplest strategies is to keep a time journal. The time journal will help you utilize your time more effectively.

The first step is to audit your time. Keep a written journal for one week (a full seven-day period). Divide each day into blocks of thirty minutes or an hour and write down what you are doing throughout the day. At the end of the seven days, review what activities you spent time on. Do you notice some blocks of time that were not very productive? Do you notice any patterns? For instance, I have found that I am very productive in the afternoon but it takes me a while to get going in the morning. With this knowledge, I am able to work on eliminating the time wasters that I find myself doing during the morning hours.

Whenever you feel you may not be using your time effectively you may want to repeat this exercise. Over the course of my career, I have returned to this journaling exercise on several occasions and every time I did it, I was able to make room for additional personal growth activities. I was always surprised at how time wasters always crept back into my schedule.

Keep an open mind

Workplace superstars approach every situation with an open mind. When you are given directions by your supervisor, begin with the assumption that the supervisor has valid reasons for the directive. You may not have all the information that the supervisor has, or you may not be able to see how your activities fit into the organization's goals. However, having an open mind also means that you speak up when you don't understand the directive and ask appropriate questions to help you understand.

Keeping an open mind means displaying fair-mindedness and flexibility, as well as being receptive to new ideas. When collaborating with co-workers, seek to understand what they are saying and why they are saying it. If you are in a situation where you supervise others, it means listening to them and valuing their contributions.

Approaching every situation with an open mind makes you receptive to new ideas and fosters collaboration in the workplace. The collaborative environment between workers often leads to solutions for the problem that combine points of view, and the combination of ideas can create solutions that neither of you have considered. This leads to better performance, greater confidence, and higher job satisfaction.

Admit mistakes and learn from them

Many people think that admitting when they are wrong is a sign of weakness, so they tend to make excuses or deflect blame when something goes wrong. Taking that approach often compounds the problem and makes the mistake more difficult to correct. No one is completely infallible. We all make mistakes. Workplace superstars acknowledge when they make a mistake.

People who recognize when to ask for help, and ask for it when they need it, display to supervisors and coworkers that they have a commitment to doing things right. Asking the others for their suggestions, ideas, or assistance emphasizes to the group that you are a team player.

The key is to learn from our mistakes and make the appropriate adjustments. Continuous course correction is the sign of an effectively functioning workplace. No one is comfortable admitting they made a mistake, but people who are open and honest with their team generate respect and foster cooperation.

Find a work mentor

Are there individuals in your organization who impress you? Get to know them. Observe how they interact with others. Learn what makes them effective in their positions. Use them as role models. Seek out someone in your organization who will agree to serve as a mentor. These mentorship relationships are not only an excellent way to gain leadership expertise, but they will provide you greater visibility in the organization and enhance your reputation.

The first person to look for as a mentor is your direct supervisor. He or she has a vested interest in your success because it helps them be successful. There may also be other people in your organization who can serve as mentors. Possibly someone in a different department would enable you to learn more about how all the functions of the organization work together. Think about what you want to learn and ask your supervisor for recommendations.

Volunteer for the unpleasant tasks (make sure they are jobs you can do) and do them well

Is there a complicated report that no one else wants to tackle? Is there a public speaking assignment that no one wants to undertake? Does someone need help re-arranging their office furniture? Does a newcomer need a tour of the facilities or a training session? Is there a special project that will have to be done quickly? These are the jobs that I would often raise my hand and volunteer for.

In every organization there are jobs that no one wants to do. These jobs may be physically demanding, they may be time-consuming, or they may simply be tedious, but they still need to be done. Throughout my career, I regularly stepped up when my supervisor asked for a volunteer, I never avoided an assignment, even when it was not something I was excited to do. In doing so, I sometimes learned new skills, I always felt a sense of accomplishment, and I became highly regarded by others in the organization.

However, it isn't necessary that you offer to take on these optional assignments every time they arise. You should be thoughtful in volunteering. Make sure the job is one that you are capable of accomplishing. You should be confident that you have the skillset to accomplish the task, and also make sure you have the time available to take it on. In addition, if you volunteer for every optional unpleasant assignment, others may just assume you will always take them on, even when it is not a good idea for you to do it.

Look for opportunities to stretch your organizational knowledge and experience

When I oversaw the student affairs function at a private college, my expertise was about all the ways that we could support the students, and how we could increase the likelihood of their success at the institution and after graduation. I was well versed in the latest theories and practices in all the aspects of student support, from housing, student life, and counseling to career development.

In the interest of my personal growth, I took advantage of every opportunity I could to work with the other departments of the college. I volunteered to teach a class so that I would be kept up to date with classroom techniques. I served on a committee that supported Director of Human Resources, and I also volunteered to work on a committee with the Admissions Department. By learning what was happening in the other departments, I was able to work collaboratively with the entire administration. I believe my career growth in the organization was positively influenced by the cross-functional knowledge and connections I made.

The more you learn about all of the aspects of your organization's operation, the more valuable you are as an employee or manager. Seek out ways to learn about what the other departments are doing. Look at what determines their success and what problems arise that they have to deal with. Tell your supervisor of your interest in learning about the other departments and ask for suggestions.

Make cross-departmental connections so that you are familiar with what is happening in the other departments. Look for committees to join or reach out to someone from another department to ask if you can job-shadow them. Depending on the nature of your job, this cross-functional outreach may require you to put in additional hours so that your own responsibilities do not suffer, but, in the long run, the time you put in will be worth it.

Make and follow a checklist for tasks that may be routine but are important

Occasionally, when I am making one of my favorite dishes for dinner, I decide to wing it without checking the recipe. I assume that, since I have made the dish dozens of times before, I have the steps memorized. When I try to cook it without referring back to the recipe, I often forget an ingredient or do the steps out of order. I will end up with something that may be edible but just doesn't taste right. The recipe that I follow is just a checklist, and by using the checklist I am able to make the dish to perfection.

When you are working in a new situation or following a procedure that you are unfamiliar with, you most likely use a checklist. However, in your personal and work life, you probably have many routine tasks that you have completed many times. A checklist is also a valuable tool for those tasks no matter how many times you have done them.

No competent airplane pilot would begin a flight without going through the pre-flight checklist, even if he or she has flown that same plane hundreds of times. The checklist ensures that everything is in place for a safe flight. A well-crafted checklist can also serve as a "what if" guide. By considering all the things that could go wrong, and including contingency plans to address them, will dramatically increase your chance for success.

Use a daily to-do list

Time management has always been a struggle for me. I often start on a task but then I realize I have a more urgent task that I am neglecting. At times, I would get to the end of my workday and realize that I neglected to do something that was important because I had been focusing on less important jobs.

I eventually realized that the solution to this problem was to write out a daily to-do list. I would make sure I listed the things that I needed accomplish that day. Not only does the list serve as a guide to ensure that I am doing what is important, I can also cross off the items as I accomplish them, so I always know where I stand in regard to what I needed to do.

Make a daily to-do list. Write down what you want to accomplish, and also write down the times during the day that you are going to work on each task. If possible, block off a few minutes at the beginning of the day when you can really focus and write out your plan. The list can be as short or as extensive as you need it to be.

However, if you make it too long, it may lead to frustration when you are unable to accomplish everything on the list.

Display a "can-do" attitude

Workplace superstars strive to always display a positive attitude. One of the qualities that supervisors have mentioned to me was my being open to take on any assignment that I was given. At times the assignments were uncomfortable for me and, at other times, they required a lot of effort to complete. I feel that my positive attitude was responsible for much of my advancement throughout my career. Even when I wasn't sure if I had the skills, I gladly accepted difficult assignments because I knew it would give me an opportunity to learn something new.

For example, when I had been a restaurant manager for less than a year, I was assigned to open a new restaurant that was under construction. I had never been in the situation before where I had to develop a plan to ensure that supplies would be ordered, people would be hired and trained, and the community would be made aware of our upcoming enterprise. The company had no guidelines, so it was up to me to figure it out. It was a successful opening, and I feel my positive attitude was, in large part responsible for the success.

Workplace superstars display a positive attitude even in difficult times. They are open to new learning experiences and they do not shy away from the hard assignments. A positive attitude can also be contagious. Often when I was working on teams, I found that when I was confident and optimistic, others would follow my lead and the entire team would work together more productively.

CHAPTER TWO – CREATE A SATISFYING WORK LIFE

A satisfying work life does not happen by accident. To gain the most satisfaction from your career, you must make purposeful choices and take actions based on these choices. Some people are blessed in that they know exactly what they want to do early in life, and they find a fulfilling career path that gives them what they seek in life. My friend Steve was that type of person. He knew early in his life that he wanted to be an eye doctor. He focused his studies and spent his entire career as an eye specialist. He found that the work was rewarding and never felt a desire to do anything else. My career path was completely different from Steve's.

I had no idea what type of a career I wanted. I switched majors more than once in college and took a variety of courses outside my major to try to find my calling. However, when I needed to find a job, I happened upon a restaurant management position and took it just to make some money. I thought it would be a temporary job until I figured out what I really wanted to do. More than a decade later I found myself still working in the restaurant industry and hating it more each day. It was easy to just get stuck in a rut and making a change seemed daunting.

One day, the frustration finally became overwhelming and I quit. I spent time re-evaluating my life and thinking about what a satisfying work life would be for me. The purposeful process led me to transition into the field of education. I found that I was a good teacher and the work gave me a sense of purpose and fulfillment that I did not get in the restaurant industry.

In my experience, I have learned that many people are like I was. They find that their work is adequate to pay their bills but it is not providing what they want to get out of life. I have seen statistics showing that on the average people may change occupations as many as three to five times during their career. That tells me that many people are searching for a better work experience. Studies have found that people who think of their work as a calling rather than simply a job are more satisfied, more engaged, and more productive in the work place.

Fortunately, you don't have to be stuck in a career that is devoid of satisfaction. I learned that if you make the effort, you can create a work situation that is rewarding and enjoyable. It is hard work and uncomfortable at times but you can succeed just as I have. I don't regret my struggles in jobs that I didn't find fulfilling because it was a good learning experience. However, you can take steps to ensure you do not find yourself in an unsatisfying position for as long as I did. Here are the actions you can take to create the work life that gives you what you are seeking.

Determine what is important to you

The process of creating a satisfying work life must include a consideration about your life outside of work. I once was working at a job that I was comfortable doing and found a degree of fulfillment, however it required me to live in a town that both my wife and I hated. We had no close friends there and we found the climate unbearable. For me, the environment outside of work eventually influenced my decision that, no matter how much I liked the job, I could never feel that any job satisfaction I was feeling could overcome the dissatisfaction with the location. I began looking at my options and quickly found a similar job in a different location that was much more to my liking.

Spend time giving serious thought to what is important to you. Do you have a preference about where you live? Many people I know have a passionate connection to the place where they are living. Maybe they have a strong attachment to friends and family living there, or they have an emotional connection that is important. Other people are more satisfied with a nomadic type of life, and they don't have a deep preference for a particular place.

Think about what is significant to you in your life. Think of past successes and what made you proud. What have they been? Examples of personal successes could be that you completed a 5k run, you completed a craft project, or you helped with a successful school fundraiser. In you work, you may have come up with a creative solution for a problem, or you may have received positive recognition from your supervisor for something that you did.

Use the knowledge you gain though this self-reflection to being making a plan. You will not be able to create a satisfying work life if your interests outside of work do not match what the work allows you to do.

Take an interest inventory – find the overlap with work

Think about what makes you happy in life. Do you enjoy hiking in a natural setting? Do cultural attractions inspire you? Are you excited by a night of dining and dancing? Do you feel a sense of contentment when you are helping a child learn something new? Looking at the types of activities that bring you joy are key to understanding what type of work you will find fulfilling. Make a list of what you like to do and write a sentence about why each entry on the list is important.

Creating a satisfying work life becomes much easier when the type of work you do and the nature of the organization you work for is related in some way to your life interests. Does your job allow you to do the things that you enjoy?

For example, I have always enjoyed traveling to new places and meeting people from different cultures. For many years, my restaurant career rarely gave me the time off that would accommodate international travel. As time went on, my frustration grew and my inability to travel was one of the major frustrations with that career. When I transitioned to a job in higher education, I was able to utilize break times between semesters to indulge in my desire for travel. The ability to accommodate my personal interests while doing work I found meaningful was an important factor in my job satisfaction.

Decide what is important – you may have to compromise at times

When thinking about ways to create a satisfying work life, you will often find you need to make trade-offs. When my children were very young, it was important to me that I have a job that had adequate salary and benefits to provide a safe and secure home for my family. I was not particularly happy in the organization that I worked for but, at that point in my life, providing for my growing family was more important than enjoying my job.

At that point in my life, I accepted that the fulfillment I would feel through my work was not solely determined by what I was doing on the job. I was able to create job satisfaction by recognizing that what I was able to accomplish for my family was important to me.

At times, you have to make choices. Can the satisfaction and fulfillment you get from the job come from what your job allows you to do and accomplish outside of work? Sometimes it can. Ideally, you want to find a career and organization that is rewarding in and of itself, while also supporting your life choices. However, you also have to weigh all the factors in your life to determine if the job is providing you what you need.

Craft meaning into your current job

If you are working at a job or career that is not very fulfilling but, for some reason, you may not be able to leave the position, then an alternative strategy is to find ways to make your current job more meaningful. Crafting meaning into your job is a deliberate process. You can change the boundaries of your job so that it will be more meaningful to you. Three possible strategies that you may employ are to change the tasks, change your relationships, or engage in cognitive crafting (changing the way you think about the job).

Change the tasks. In some situations you may be able to modify your work process. Think about what is important to you and take steps to change what you are doing to make the work more satisfying. If possible, take on more of the tasks that are important to you. Or endeavor to restrict the tasks that do not lead to satisfaction by seeking ways to delegate them. In addition, you may be able to change the order in which you do things to make it more meaningful.

Look at where you have a degree of freedom to make the changes. You may be able to customize the experience to make it more enjoyable or meaningful. You may have to negotiate with superiors to make the adjustments. Ask yourself, "What does the organization expect me to accomplish?" Then seek ways to ensure you are accomplishing what the organization wants while making the tasks a better fit for you.

Recraft your relationships with others in the workplace. Our relationships with other people is usually the source of our greatest joy or our greatest frustration. Seek out individuals who exemplify the positive attitudes about the job that you want to develop. Talk to the people you encounter on the job. Ask them about what it is that makes the job rewarding to them. As much as possible, surround yourself with people who demonstrate a positive attitude about the work they are doing.

The tactic that you have the most direct control over is to engage in cognitive crafting, and it can be a powerful tool to help discover or create meaning in the work you are doing. Consider the following questions. What are the benefits to the recipients of your service or product? How does what you are doing make life better for others? When you answer those questions, you begin see yourself in a different relationship with the tasks you do. You begin to change your attitude about the work. The job satisfaction comes from how you impart meaning into what you are doing.

Seek a positive work environment

An important factor in job satisfaction is feeling comfortable with your co-workers and with the overall environment in the organization. A toxic organizational atmosphere will be detrimental to one's work-life satisfaction no matter how rewarding the actual job duties are. Twice in my career, I found myself working for horrible bosses. In both cases, I was doing work that I found rewarding and enjoyable. However, the atmosphere in each workplace changed dramatically when a new supervisor took over.

In each case, the new supervisor was disparaging, condescending, and disrespectful to employees, often in front of other employees. The tension created in these negative workplace situations led to poor performance and high employee turnover. I found my anxiety levels rising every day as I prepared to go to work. In both situations, I decided to leave the organization.

Finding a positive work environment is an important factor in creating a satisfying work life. In my experience, it was better for me to leave the job than to put up with the negativity. In some cases, you may be in a position to create a positive work experience even when there are negative people in the organization. The key is to develop relationships with the positive people whom you work with and keep focused on the rewarding aspects of the work. However, keep in mind that there may be times when your only good recourse is to move on.

Remain open to new possibilities

Often the best opportunities come when you least expect them. While things may be going well in your current situation, there is always the possibility that better opportunities will arise. It is important to keep in mind that the world is constantly changing, and the pace of change continues to increase. My adult offspring are working in companies and doing tasks that didn't exist when I was starting out.

Keep track of what is happening in the fields that interest you. Learn about the newest developments that affect your current job. Tasks that were done manually a decade ago are now automated, and this creates new opportunities for individuals who are paying attention to the industry trends. New industries are constantly popping up and the chances are great that new possibilities will arise in your work.

Keep an open mind about the other things in life that interest you. I have enjoyed exploring new places and meeting new people since I was young. I was fortunate to eventually find a job that allowed me the time to travel internationally on a regular basis. However, I was never able to turn my love of travel into a career. I thought about becoming a freelance writer about travel, but the whole process of mailing story proposal letters to publishers and waiting weeks for a response did not appeal to me. Today, the process has become streamlined with online publications and email communication. Technology has transformed the industry and I am now enjoying a career that wasn't feasible for me ten or fifteen years ago.

Keep looking at what is happening in the world around you. New possibilities are likely to arise that you should consider. By keeping an open mind you might be surprised at the options that appear. You may discover new opportunities for creating a satisfying work life that you hadn't considered. Whether it is moving on to a new organization or discovering ways to make your current job even more satisfying, always be vigilant.

Create balance in your life

A satisfying work life goes hand-in-hand with balance outside your work life. Even when you are doing a job that you love to do, if you spend all of your time at work, constantly thinking about work even when you are off duty, you may experience frustration and regret about what you are missing. Your work life will be more fulfilling when you are able to find the best ratio for you between work time and non-work activities.

One of the least satisfying positions I held in my career was with a good organization, the work was enjoyable and the compensation was good. However, I was required to be on call twenty four hours a day and seven days a week. Although I wasn't actually putting in an excessive number of hours, the unpredictability meant that I could never feel like I was not at work. My satisfaction with that job deteriorated because I resented the lack of balance.

Determining the work-life balance that is optimal for you takes some work. You have to give thorough consideration to what you really want out of life and set limits on your time. Make a list of what is important to you. Is it being able to attend family events? Is it taking the time to exercise? Create a schedule that will allow you to accomplish your goals and stick to it. Determine how you can set boundaries between work and home. Decide when you can say no to extra tasks that take up time but are not necessary.

Every job can be made more satisfying by developing a system to separate your work life and your personal life. If you feel frustrated and dissatisfied at work, it might not necessarily be the job itself. Creating an appropriate balance between your job and your outside life may help create a satisfied life ever without changing jobs.

Create a satisfying work life by using the WOOP method

Throughout my life I have always been an optimistic person. I have a positive outlook on life even when things are not going well. This positive outlook has enabled me to continually move forward in my work life. Early in my career I learned about the power of setting goals and delighted in seeing them coming to fruition. I read about how to accomplish one's goals and attended countless lectures and workshops about the topic.

One step that many of the self-improvement gurus describe is to visualize that you have already accomplished your goals. I tried visualization many times and it never seemed to make any difference. The things that I visualized never came about. Then I learned that simply visualizing your goals is not enough, and I began to look for what else I needed to do beyond imagining that my goals would be accomplished.

I realized that the process I came to use is now called WOOP. It stands for wish, objective, obstacle and plans. This process takes you beyond simply visualizing what you want. The process goes like this: choose a challenging and realistic goal that you want to achieve (Wish); imagine the best possible outcome that will result from accomplishing that goal (Outcome); visualize the obstacles that may stand in the way of you accomplishing the objective (Obstacle); and then make a plan to overcome those obstacles (Plan).

By using the WOOP method, you have a focused approach to creating the life you want. We often are stopped for accomplishing our goals because we had not given any thought to the obstacles that might arise. By using WOOP, we are prepared for the obstacles and have a plan in place to overcome them.

Recognize that your work life is a constantly evolving process

One important lesson I have learned as I reflect on the jobs and careers that I have had is that things change. One organization in which I felt my work responsibilities were enjoyable and fulfilling was suddenly purchased by a larger organization that had a different company culture and overall goals that I could not feel good about supporting. I stuck with the job for a while but I was not happy, and I quickly went about finding a position with an organization that was more closely aligned with my thinking.

It is important to accept the fact that circumstances beyond your control can, and invariably will, intrude on your life plans, and you have to make adjustments. When those circumstances arise, you have a choice. You can let outside factors chart your course, or you can take control and modify the situation. By taking control of the process, you will be able to find your calling, however you define it.

CHAPTER THREE – FIND A MEANINGFUL CAREER

By the end of our working life, most of us will have spent several decades on the job. Unfortunately, the vast majority of individuals lead lives of quiet frustration, toiling away in an organization or career that provides little satisfaction or fulfillment. Finding a career that is rewarding can occasionally happen by chance, but taking a well-planned approach significantly increases the likelihood for success in this search for a meaningful and rewarding work situation.

I know how it feels to be in a career that I was not suited for. I floated along for many years in an unsatisfying career. I was very successful in that career, but I was frustrated. The jobs I had allowed me to pay my bills but they left me feeling empty and dissatisfied. It was only when I began the deliberate process of determining where I wanted my career to take me that I found a fulfilling career.

I know some people who simply happened to land in a career that was made for them. However, for most of us, the path to a meaningful career is circuitous, and often leads to several dead ends before we find what we are seeking. The key to landing in a meaningful career is to never give up. If you keep at it, you will find what you are meant to do.

Be purposeful – don't just go with the flow

It is easy to get lulled into a situation where you feel stuck. That happened to me, and I am pretty sure it happens to a large portion of the population. Finding a career that is fulfilling will not happen unless you make a conscious decision to develop a plan and move into a better situation.

When I was just out of college, I took the first job I could find – as an assistant manager at a local restaurant. At that time I was just looking for a job that would pay the bills. I figured that I would work there for a short time while I decided what type of a career I really wanted. I was never passionate about the work. To me it was just a job, and I assumed it was something I could put up with for a while but it wouldn't be permanent. My plan did not work out quite the way I thought it would. I was good enough at the job to be promoted to higher levels of management. I found myself in a career field that paid well, and I grew to be comfortable doing it. However, deep inside I knew I really wanted more than that for my life.

It was many years before I finally realized I needed to move on to a new career field. While I was comfortable, I felt that other careers would bring greater satisfaction and a stronger feeling of fulfillment. It seemed easier to just keep doing what I was doing in that job than to do the work of deciding what I felt I was really meant to do.

Eventually, I got to a point where my frustration was too serious for me to ignore. I still remember the moment when I made the decision to take purposeful action. I conducted a self-analysis and researched possible careers. After months of work, I had developed a plan that would allow me to transition out of a career I hated and into one that was a perfect fit. The specific process is different for everyone but, unless you take a deliberate focused approach, your chance of success is slim.

Consider your interests when looking at potential careers

When you are considering a possible career, think about what activities you like spending time doing. What hobbies do you find engaging? What do you read about? What internet sites are most interesting to you? Do you enjoy mingling with others at large gatherings? Are you more at ease with a small group of friends or are you most comfortable indulging in quiet time at home?

When your career is aligned with your interests, job satisfaction is more likely. Not all hobbies or enjoyable interests can be developed into a successful career but most can. When you are looking for a new situation, start with what you enjoy doing. Then do the research. Look into what types of careers are associated with the activities you enjoy and determine if any of them are right for you. I know people who loved collecting trading cards and were able to turn their interest into a lucrative business. Another person who was captivated by athletic shoes from a young age has found a successful career with a large athletic apparel organization. The story is the same for many individuals that I know. They were able to transition a passion into a fulfilling career.

Think about what you hate doing and avoid it

It may seem obvious, but many people spend years slogging their way through life in a career doing jobs that they hate doing. There are some types of jobs that I don't like to do. I once thought that I might want to be an accountant. I have good mathematical skills and understand the concepts well enough to teach beginning courses in accounting. However, I am not particularly detail oriented and when I gave it serious consideration, I realized I would be extremely frustrated and dissatisfied at that type of job. I abhor sitting behind a desk all day. Even when I had a job that required time in the office, I found as many excuses as I could to get out of the office and walk around. I realized that we spend too much of our lives working in our career to allow ourselves to get stuck in a job that we hate doing.

I have a friend who breaks into a sweat and gets butterflies in his stomach when he even thinks about talking in front of a group of people. Like many individuals, he finds that public speaking is a very uncomfortable situation. He aspired to a career that would allow him to help others learn and grow. He actually became a teacher even though he struggled giving lectures.

My friend thought he would always be stuck in a career that he was meant to do but was emotionally and physically uncomfortable for him. He stuck with the classroom career for a long time because he felt it was the best way to help other people. But he hated it. When he finally decided to leave the position, he began to work in online education. His new position eliminated his public speaking frustration, allowed him to continue doing what he was good at doing and increased his feeling of fulfillment.

Stay away from a career that requires you to do jobs that you hate doing. If you find yourself continually frustrated, it is a good sign that there is a better career out there for you. There are way too many opportunities for a satisfying career for you to languish in one filled with frustration and anxiety.

Think about the types of physical environment and activities that you do enjoy

The physical environment in which you work and the type of physical activities that your job requires will have a profound effect on how you feel about the job. For example, I have always enjoyed the outdoors. I have discovered that when I find myself working at the computer for several hours at a time, I become frustrated no matter how well I enjoy the work that I am doing. I need to take regular fresh-air breaks in order to maintain my productivity. A meaningful career to me meant one that allowed me the opportunity to spend at least some time out of doors.

Think about the type of work schedule that you would be comfortable with. When I was in restaurant management, my schedule included early morning shifts and late evening shifts. The varying schedule and the requirement to work either early in the morning or late into the evening was one of the things I liked least about the job. On top of that, it was very difficult to take a vacation because I could not be away from the job for more than a few days at a time. When I decided to leave that career, I purposely transitioned to a new field that had regular hours. It provided a lot more free time and I was able to schedule my time off more advantageously.

Play to your strengths

Your career will be much more satisfying to you when you play to your strengths. Do the type of work that utilizes your skills and abilities. Make a list completing the statement "I am good at..." with as many words and phrases as you can think of. Don't limit the list and don't prejudge. You may not be able to think of a career offhand that uses your particular skillset, but it is out there.

What have you received recognition or praise for? For example, have others noticed that you are good at solving problems? Have you received praise because you are good at following detailed directions? Are you able to successfully explain complex ideas to others so they understand them?

Use this information to develop a list of the skills, abilities, and knowledge that you already possess. This list can also benefit from feedback by others. Sometimes we don't recognize our strengths but others may provide insight. Ask them what they think you are good at. You may be surprised. When I first completed this exercise, friends noted that I was very good at teaching people new things. I had never considered myself as a teacher or trainer until then.

Thinking about what you are good at, is the best place to start when seeking a meaningful career. However, realize that you don't solely have to rely on what knowledge you already have. It is never too late to learn new skills and gain new knowledge to supplement what you already have.

Think about transferrable skills and fusion of skills

Your meaningful career choices should not be limited to what may seem as the most obvious areas. Think about what skills you have. The skills, knowledge and abilities that you already possess can often be appropriate for many different types of careers.

When I realized that I was adept at teaching and training, I found many avenues to explore. My skill was being able to explain complex processes in a simple fashion so it would be easy to understand. I realized that I could use that skill in a corporate training situation, I could develop independent workshops as an entrepreneur, or I could go into a more formal educational setting.

You already have a wide variety of skills that can be applied to any field. Here are some skills that you may already possess that can potentially be valuable in any field: oral communication, public speaking, written communication, leadership or management experience, computer skills, research competency, project management, time management, conflict resolution (mediation), fluency in a foreign language, and organizational skills.

Think about what you are good at doing, but avoid thinking about it in terms of a particular company or industry. Are you good at solving problems? Are adept at paying attention to details? Have you been recognized for your creative thinking? These qualities can lead to success in a variety of careers. If you have identified a particular career field that you are interested in, take an inventory of your skills and accomplishments, and then look for ways that they can be utilized in that new career.

You do not want to limit yourself to skills you use at work. Consider all your activities. Activities such as organizing a fund drive for a volunteer organization, founding a club or discussion group, working on projects for a service organization, and teaching at a community center are examples of activities that highlight your personal skills. Whether you realize it or not, you have a wide array of skills and experiences that are transferrable to nearly any workplace.

Think about what you are <u>not</u> good at doing

There are many career fields that may sound interesting and that may be lucrative but they do not match your skills, abilities, or personality. Are you the type of person who is very detail oriented? Or are you more of a big-picture thinker? Are you a self-starter who can work effectively without any supervision? Or do you work best when you are the member of a team?

For example, I once thought about doing scientific research as a career. However, a career as a researcher would not be a great choice for me. While I am good with numbers and have a deep understanding of science and math principles, I am not an extremely detailed person. I would have little patience for the kind of detailed work that a researcher is called upon to do.

Take time to think about your personality. Some careers are made to order for extroverts. Other fields are not suitable for in introvert. Being an introvert, I am much more comfortable writing than I am at presenting a sales pitch. You may want to think about the types of activities that you are not suited to do and avoid them. Within every workplace, there are different types of jobs. Some will be more suited to your personality and skills, while there are others that you will want to avoid.

Brainstorm possibilities with people you trust

Look to people who know you and regularly interact with you for suggestions. The people close to you can provide valuable insight into what you are good at doing and what you are not as good at. When I was contemplating a mid-life career change, I interviewed several people whom I knew. I wanted to get their perceptions about my strengths, and to hear any recommendations they might have. These were people whom I interacted with in a variety of situations, but they were all individuals I was confident would give me unbiased advise and solid recommendations.

With the exception of my spouse, I avoided asking my family members for advice. In my case, I was not sure they would be objective. So be careful about the family members who you approach. At times, they can be an excellent resource, while at other times, family dynamics may affect their feedback. I found that, for me, outside the family was better because they were more likely to be objective.

You may or may not want to talk to people who you currently work with. In my case, I did not want the company to know that I was thinking of transitioning to something new, so I avoided talking to co-workers. I did consult with a former co-worker. He had been a valuable mentor when we worked together, and he had moved on to a new organization so I was comfortable asking him. He was not only willing to provide excellent advice, he was very encouraging in support of my endeavor.

Recruit a personal board of advisors

Nearly all successful businesses have an advisory board of some type. It is generally comprised of people who are not involved in the day-to-day operation of the business. They act as an objective outside resource to provide feedback and offer suggestions. A personal board of advisors operates in the same way. You can meet with them to discuss your plans and hear their suggestions. It may take a bit of work to recruit this board of advisors but the payoff will be well worth the work.

Many successful business leaders are happy to help give feedback to people interested in entering the field. On occasion, I filled this role for people who had been my students and wanted my advice about industries they were interested in.

Identify a handful of individuals, generally no more than three or four, who are successful in the field that you are interested in transitioning to and approach them. Successful people are often very busy, so you may have to approach several before you find a few who are willing to do it. You may want to invite them to have coffee with you or even give them a dinner invitation. Let them know that this will be a group discussion and not one-on-one. To be respectful of their time, you want to treat this as a business meeting. Prepare an agenda and keep the conversation focused on your transition objectives. Ask for their advice, criticism and recommendations about your transition plan.

Look at the market demand

When I was beginning my work life, I was enthralled by a book that was popular at the time. The premise of the book is that money will follow if you choose the type of work you love to do. That sounded great to me. What I eventually realized was that doing what you love was only half of the process.

You need to couple doing what you love to do with doing what someone will pay you for doing. I could think of many things that I loved to do were really only suitable for me as hobbies. I loved spending time hiking and camping, I loved taking pictures, I loved reading and learning new things, and I enjoyed traveling and exploring new places. All of those activities were wonderful hobbies but, at that time, there were very few ways I could think of that these activities were marketable. I learned that I needed to look for ways to integrate what I loved to do with what I was skilled at and what would be a viable profession.

The other question you should ask yourself is whether you would still enjoy that activity if you were to do it as a full-time job. I loved to cook for my friends and family, and I was pretty good at it. However, when I was working in restaurant management, I learned what being a restaurant chef would entail.

I realized that spending eight or more hours a day constantly cooking would quickly turn into drudgery. Maybe I would have eventually made a decent living but, for me, cooking would no longer be an activity I loved to do. It would be the perfect life for some people but not for me. In addition, I realized that the demand for high-quality chefs in any particular market is pretty limited.

I also loved photography. During and immediately after college I spent most of my free time roaming the country photographing the beauty of nature. I thought it would be a wonderful career. However, there were only a handful of really successful nature photographers in the entire country, so breaking into that field was nearly impossible. To learn about the field of photography, I worked for a short time for a portrait photographer. I learned that there was a great demand for photographing people and events but, as much as I loved photography, I learned that doing wedding photography and portrait photography was not what I enjoyed. I came to realize that what the market wanted and what I wanted to do were not in synch. So I stayed away from a career in photography.

Make a purposeful transition: Determine what careers and jobs are a good fit for you

If you are not sure what type of a career is the best fit, do your research. Informational interviews are an excellent way to find out about potential careers. I have used them successfully during my times of transition.

Begin the process by brainstorming the types of careers you are interested in researching. Then look at companies or organizations doing the kind of work you are interested in. Once you have narrowed the search to a couple organizations, look for someone in the organization who is doing the type of work you would like to find out about and contact them to ask for an interview.

When you contact them, stress that you are merely seeking an informational interview to learn more about what they do in their job. Make it clear that you are not asking for an employment interview, but simply interested in learning more about the type of work they do. I have found that nearly all the people I have approached were happy to give me some time to talk about their work (I usually asked for fifteen minutes).

When you go to the interview, observe everything you can about the work and about the workplace. Take note of the workplace environment. Be prepared with a list of questions. Topics such as the day-to-day activities that the position entails, how much independence someone in that role has, what is satisfying about the job, what types of career paths are likely, what frustrations come with the job, and what are the essential skills someone in that position needs to in order to be successful will provide important information. Ask the person you are interviewing about their career path and for any recommendations they may have to someone interested in entering the field.

In some cases, you may be able to find an opportunity to try out a similar job before you fully launch yourself into a career. Some organizations offer internship opportunities while others may have part-time positions available. Looking for these types of opportunities will allow you get a flavor of the job without making a full-time commitment.

You can also look for volunteer opportunities. Non-profit organizations and associations have wide varieties of types of positions you can volunteer for. When I was thinking about becoming an accountant. I volunteered to be the financial officer for a small local service organization. That position only took a few hours a month but I was able to get a glimpse at the activities of an accountant. When I was researching a career in photography, I took a part-time job with a local photographer. I arranged a flexible schedule that didn't interfere with my full-time job while I learned about the field. From those two activities, I learned that I was not suited to an accounting or photography career.

The more information you can gather about potential careers that interest you, the more smoothly your transition will be. Jumping into a job opportunity without doing in-depth research often results in going from on job that you don't like to a new job that you find just as unsatisfactory.

Conquer the fear of transition

Transitions can be hard to implement. Over the course of my working career, I made three major transition. In those instances, I not only changed my workplace, I entered entirely new fields that were unrelated to my prior career. Each time, I was apprehensive. Transitioning into a new career brings a lot of risks. You have to learn new skills, and you may find yourself in a different environment.

The most important tactic is to make it a purposeful process. Plan out what you will need to do and begin implementing the plan. For me, the plan took shape over the course of several months. I recognized that it was time to move on to a different career, then I began the transition process before leaving my old job. Here are strategies you can use to make the transition less intimidating.

Learn all you can before you make the move. If your reluctance is rooted in a feeling that you don't know what it will take to be successful in the new career, you can address that. Take a class to learn about the areas where your knowledge is lacking. For example, if you want to become better with finance, take a math class or an accounting course at a local community college. Educational resources are available in nearly every community. If you can't find what you need locally, check out online courses. You can find a course about any topic online.

How you talk to yourself can have a strong influence on how confident you are as you make the transition. It may be hard at times to tell yourself you can do something when you are unsure if you can, but when you keep repeating to yourself that you will be successful, your odds for success increase. Listen to your internal voice and pay attention to the times when negative thoughts arise. When those negative thoughts arise, you have to attack them with a positive response. When you think "I can't do this," change it to "I have a solid plan, and I will do this."

Recognize and give yourself credit for the successes you have already had. Confidence comes from recognizing your abilities and taking action even in difficult circumstances. Nothing builds self-confidence better than success. Keep track of your successes. When you review the progress toward your transition, you should pay particular attention to the success you have had in prior careers. We often gloss over our accomplishments and focus on the things that went wrong.

While you want to recognize the areas where improvement is needed, it is even more important to celebrate what went right and realize that you can repeat your successes in the new environment. Even though it may have been gained in a different career, or in a different type of workplace, you have gained valuable work experience that will serve you well in your new career.

Don't limit yourself

When I was in my twenties, having just graduated from college, I had a wide variety of interests. I loved photography, I enjoyed writing, I appreciated art and, most of all, I loved to travel to new places and immerse myself in new experiences. Wow, I had a lot of potential careers in those topics that I enjoyed. Unfortunately, I lacked the confidence to try to make any of those activities into a career. I didn't even make an effort to enter any of the fields that I dreamed about.

It took a couple of decades for me to realize that I was not giving myself permission to try the things I dreamed about. When I finally allowed myself to overcome the limits I had placed on my dreams, I was able to move forward. Since then, I have traveled all over the world, lived in foreign countries, and strengthened my photography and writing skills. I was able to exceed my expectations and become successful doing something I love to do.

You will never know what you are capable of until you try. History of full of examples of people who accomplished amazing things that no one, even themselves, expected them to achieve. As in the famous quote attributed to Walt Disney, "If you can dream it, you can do it," you probably have more talents and abilities than you realize.

Of course, your dreams must be accompanied by the preparation necessary to fulfill them. You may need to learn new skills to become successful, but no one is too old to learn new ways to enhance the talents that they already possess. You probably don't have to take decades to reach your dreams like I did, but my point is that you will never reach your dreams if you don't try for them.

Develop a transition plan

Good things in your career rarely happen by accident. In my experience, waiting for a great opportunity to materialize out of thin air may, on rare occasion result in positive change, However your chance of making a successful transition are greatly increased when you map out a transition plan.

For a career transition, your plan should include several topics:

1) What is your destination? You may or may not have a specific company in mind but you should determine what industry entails your dream career destination. You might be able to develop a list of several companies that offer the type of jobs you want to transition to.

2) Your plan should include a list of the knowledge, skills, and abilities that one needs to be successful in that new career. Learn as much as you can about where you want to go.

3) You should also include a realistic assessment of what new skills you will need to learn. Also determine where you will be able to fill in any holes in your knowledge and experience.

4) Finally, you need an action plan. List what steps you will take to move through your transition. How do you plan to make connections with the people and companies you are interested in?

Your transition plan can be as detailed as you want, but a written plan will keep you on track as you move through the transition. The written plan will also serve as encouragement when you inevitable have a bad day and need some encouragement.

Realize that career paths are not linear

Throughout my career, I realized the journey was never a straight line. The route was meandering. At times, I knew exactly where I was heading but at other times, I felt I was going in circles. There were often dead ends and, at other times, new roads opened that I had never imagined.

Once you recognize and admit that there will be times when not everything is going great, it will be much easier to maintain a positive attitude and to consistently take action toward your dreams. Consistent daily action will enable you to move forward in your career, even when you do not seem to be making progress.

It is also important to note that the workplace is constantly evolving. My two sons are working in careers that did not even exist when they were born. They prepared themselves with the skillsets that were increasingly becoming in demand and found ways to leverage their skills into dream jobs with their dream companies. You want to keep exploring, learn about the trends and keep abreast with the new technologies.

Be persistent

The key to a successful career transition is persistence. You may not end up in your ideal job on the first attempt. You may have to take interim steps. Maybe you can do volunteer work to meet people in the industry. Maybe you will look for an internship. Maybe you will have to take an entry-level job with a company in the industry you aspire to.

Do not be frustrated if you have to pace yourself as you transition. Actually, easing your way into a new career by taking a steady approach may be less stressful in the long run. While it sounds great to immediately jump into the position and/or company that you have dreamed of, you are more likely to set yourself up for long term success when you proceed at a measured pace. Continue to take steps to gain the skills and experience that will lead you forward and persistently move toward your goal.

Keep looking for personal growth opportunities and keep learning as much as you can. Seek out ways to network with people already doing what you would like to do, such as online forums or industry-wide organizations. The more visible you are, the more opportunities you will find coming your way.

CHAPTER FOUR – OVERCOME OBSTACLES TO YOUR SUCCESS

The first three chapters of this book teach you how to become more successful. Whether you want to become better at your current job, find new opportunities in your current career or transition to a different career altogether, you will be able to map out a successful plan.

For most of us, we often miss opportunities because of the obstacles that we think are holding us back. At times, the obstacles are external, for example when we need more training. However, many of the obstacles we encounter are internal. We unwittingly create roadblocks for ourselves.

You may have doubts about your ability to succeed, or you might have a tendency to procrastinate. Poor time management can derail the best-laid plans, and excuses can slow down progress. No matter what your goals in life are, it is important that you keep in mind the internal obstacles that hold you back. Know that they can appear at any time, and be prepared to counteract them. Taking positive steps, such as those described in the following pages will enable you to conquer those internal obstacles to your success.

Build a Positive Mindset to eliminate excuses

Excuses for not moving forward are easy to create. "I am too old to make a career change now." "It is hard work to make the changes I need to make." "I don't have the right skills for what I want to do." "The economy is bad, and it's a poor time to make any changes." "Things may not work out the way I hope."

Over the course of my career, I have grappled with every one of these self-made excuses at one time or another. I learned that by recognizing that these excuses were simply defense mechanisms that my subconscious threw up to avoid change. We humans often struggle with making changes in our lives even though we know those changes will make our life better. It is much easier to put up with things as they are than to do what is necessary to make a change in our situation.

When I struggled with these excuses, I learned that the best way to defeat them was to create a positive mindset. The process boils down to just taking action. Take one step toward your goal. Every you time take a positive action, you begin to overcome one of the excuses that is holding you back. You become more confident, and you start building a more positive mindset. That positive mindset will carry you forward even when you experience setbacks. Setbacks will inevitably occur, but armed with a positive attitude you will continue to carry on. If you are not taking steps to move forward in your life, you will never make it to where you want to go.

Beat Procrastination in order to move forward

Okay, you have a plan, and you know what you need to do to achieve your goals, but you just can't seem to get around to working on the plan. Putting an important task off by filling your time with minor busywork, yielding to distractions, or waiting for the right time to begin are the tell-tale signs of procrastination. If you are postponing an important action for a good reason, that may be a valuable part of the process. However, putting actions off continually or avoiding doing something because it may be unpleasant can derail your progress before you start.

Generally, I am fully aware that I am procrastinating when I am in that state. For me procrastination causes a great deal of internal stress. I know I should begin the task but I find all kinds of excuses to keep from moving forward. When you find yourself procrastinating, begin by asking yourself why you are procrastinating. Is the task boring or does it lack meaning for you? Are you not sure what the next task is that you should do, or is it difficult?

Since the actions we are talking about are the steps to meet your life goals and fulfill your personal mission statement, you can begin defeating procrastination by reviewing why you embarked on this path to begin with. Think about your self-talk about the topic. Changing your inner dialogue from "I have to" to "I choose to because..." will emphasize the reasons for moving ahead. Here are strategies to break out of the procrastination rut.

Focus on the beginning rather than

the ending

The whole process may feel daunting. This is especially true when we embark on a journey of personal change. There are so many steps that you need to take in order to reach your goals that you wonder if you will ever make it through your journey to a more successful life. Combat this apprehension by focusing on starting. What is the first action you need to take? If you want to get into physical condition so that you can complete a 5K run, tell yourself "today I will begin by running for fifteen minutes."

Find an accountability partner

I absolutely hate letting others down. When I make a commitment to someone else, I do everything I can to keep that commitment. I use the same process to keep on track and avoid procrastinating. Share your goals with someone you trust. I share my plans with my spouse and family members, and that drives me to complete the tasks. I don't need to ask for their feedback or cheerleading, it is enough that I have made my intentions public. Make sure the people you share this with have a positive attitude toward your goals. You don't want a naysayer to disrupt your progress.

Just get started doing something

Commit to yourself that you will do something every day to work on your action plans. If the next action step seems intimidating, break it into smaller activities and begin work on one of those. A technique I use is to tackle the least pleasant task first. Once that is done, the more enjoyable tasks are easier to work on. You may want to revisit the action plans you made to achieve your life goals and determine which ones are the most intimidating. Work on them first.

Remove distractions

When I am mired in a period of procrastination, I become distracted easily. Whether it is email, social media or phone calls, anything that interrupts my progress can lead to a period of procrastination. To break out of a procrastination cycle, I need to shut out those disruptions. Think about what distractions you are drawn to and remove them while you work. Your emails will still be there after you have spent an hour working on your plan of action. Your social media friends will not miss you if you tune them out for a while.

Procrastination can rear its head up anytime in the process. If may stop you from beginning a project, or it may slow down your progress in the middle of the action.

The key to overcoming it is to recognize that you are procrastinating, think about why you are procrastinating, and then take purposeful steps to begin moving forward.

Time management: Make time to achieve success

A major roadblock for many people is carving out time when you have a busy schedule. If you work full time, it may seem hard to find those extra hours to work on your goals. However, the reality of the situation is that, unless you make the time, you will never achieve the success you deserve. You have spent the time creating the plan to reach your goals and to fulfill your personal mission in life. Continue the progress by using your time wisely.

Yes, it is often hard to make time to work on personal goals when you have a busy life. I know the feeling. I was working in a full-time job that demanded my total focus when I decided that the only way I could move forward on my path was to begin study in a graduate program. Working full time, attending class as a full-time student, and making time to study was difficult but I managed it. If I can do it, so can you. You have to make it a priority to use your time wisely.

Track your time usage

When I began my graduate program, I quickly learned strategies that helped me capture the time that I needed to juggle everything in my life. The first step is to audit your time. Keep a written journal for one full week (a full seven-day week). Divide the day into blocks of thirty minutes or an hour and write down what you are doing throughout the day. At the end of the seven days, review what activities you spent time on. Do you notice some blocks of time that were not very productive?

Over the course of my career, I have returned to this journaling exercise on several occasions and every time I did it, I was able to make room for additional personal growth activities. I was always surprised at how time wasters always crept back into my schedule.

Create extra pockets of time

You may want to consider creating extra time for yourself. Determine to get out of bed a half hour earlier every day to work on your action plans. Or, take thirty minutes at night before going to bed. Over a month's time, capturing an extra thirty minutes a day will add up to a substantial amount of time.

Several years ago, I began walking to improve my health. I was determined to walk at least forty-five minutes a day but, with a full time job I wasn't sure where I would find the time. When I looked at how I was spending my time, I realized that I watched television for more than an hour every night. When I thought about it, I decided that walking to improve my health was more important to me than watching television and I began an evening walking program.

Use your commuting time effectively. At times in my career, I was commuting by car for as much as fifty minutes each way. I found that listening to audio books was a simple way to use that commute for personal enrichment. When I was in graduate school, I had switched to public transportation and I was able to do the reading for my studies as I rode the bus.

Determine to use your weekend productively. You may be able to set aside time to work on your more time-consuming projects. You should also make it a priority to schedule in some rest and relaxation time on the weekend. Taking the time to recharge will allow you to be more productive when you are working toward your goals.

Exploit the power of lists

Make a daily to-do list. Write down what you want to accomplish, and also write down the times during the day that you are going to work on your personal success. Block off uninterrupted time when you can really focus. If you can't set aside a large block of time, then you may be able to find several shorter intervals that you can put to effective use.

To find time for working on your goals, you may need to consider reducing the time commitments that are currently on your schedule. Consider cutting out one activity, like I did when I cut out watching television at night. You might also consider reducing your social activities for a while. You may have to say "no" to requests from friends and family members.

Consider negotiating for time. When I was studying, I negotiated with my supervisor to adjust my work schedule. I was able to block out some times during the work day to leave work and attend class. I committed to continue to meet all my work responsibilities by working later on some days.

When I was manager of a department, I worked out an agreement with one of my employees that she would work four ten-hour days per week so she could have one day a week off to attend school. Can you work out an arrangement like that? Think about other ways to negotiate for extra time. Can you negotiate a chore-sharing arrangement with your spouse that will allow you to schedule times to work on your goals?

Don't let time constraints become an excuse for not moving forward toward your goals. It make take some thought, and you may have to be creative about it, but the time is there for you to use. You have to make it a priority to work on your success plan.

Build your confidence to move forward

One of the biggest roadblocks I have faced in my work life and in my personal life, and still face at times, is lack of confidence. The nagging questions always hang around in the back of my mind. Can I really accomplish this? What if these actions don't help me realize my goals? What if I don't succeed? I think everyone struggles with this to some degree.

I imagine that most of the people I have worked with over the years would find it hard to believe that I was struggling with self-confidence. I was able to project an air of confidence but inside I felt I was putting on an act. Even when things were not going well, I could act as if I had confidence in my actions. I believe that one of the keys to my many successes in the workplace has been my ability to keep a calm, steady, confident demeanor even when I was under tremendous stress.

Recognize your successes

Confidence comes from recognizing your abilities and taking action even in difficult circumstances. Nothing builds self-confidence better than success. Keep track of your successes. When you review the progress toward your goals, you should pay particular attention to what went right. We often gloss over our accomplishments and focus on the things that went wrong. While you want to recognize the areas where improvement is needed, it is even more important to celebrate what went right.

When you review the progress you are making toward your goals, make a list of what you did that was successful. It is a good idea to keep a written list of these accomplishments so you can refer back to them. Review this list of accomplishments often, and they will exert a positive influence on your subconscious mind when you are faced with a challenging situation.

Take concrete actions

Learn something new. If your lack of confidence is rooted in a feeling that you don't know how to be successful, you need to address that. Take a class to learn about the areas where your knowledge is lacking. For example, if you want to become better with finance, take a math class or an accounting course at a local community college. Educational resources are available in nearly every community. If you can't find what you need locally, check out online courses. You can find a course about any topic online.

Change a habit. Make it a simple, straightforward change. Set your alarm to wake you ten minutes earlier and use that ten minutes to meditate. Write down a grocery list before you go shopping. Read for ten minutes a day. Choose something small that you know you can do. Continue the new activity for a month.

Reach out of your comfort zone

Identify actions that will take you out of your comfort zone. It can be a bit scary to take on something that you are wary of, but take that step. Look at areas of your job that make you uncomfortable and take them on. Volunteer for a special project that will stretch your abilities. I have done this many times throughout my career, and I feel it has done the most to boost my self-confidence.

When I a left a successful career at an educational institution, I thought about continuing my teaching career at another local school. Instead, I opted to look for an opportunity to work in a foreign country. While it was a job I could do, moving to another country was intimidating. I was nervous at first, but I learned that I could become successful in this new situation.

You can also identify ways to reach out of your comfort zone in your non-work life. For example, I would venture to guess that most people are intimidated by speaking in public. Becoming comfortable talking in front of groups can be a real boost to their overall confidence. There are clubs, such as the Toastmasters, in every community that offer the opportunity to become skilled at public speaking.

Use positive self-talk

How you talk to yourself can have a strong influence on how confident you are. It may be hard at times to tell yourself you can do something when you are unsure if you can, but keep telling yourself you will be successful and your odds for success increase. Listen to your internal voice and pay attention to the times when negative thoughts arise. When those negative thoughts arise, you have to attack them with a positive response. When you think "I can't do this," change it to "I will do this."

Resist the urge to compare yourself with others

Every person has a set of unique skills and abilities. When you compare yourself to others, you lose sight of what you are good at. Learn what your strengths are and use them to your advantage. Learn what areas you want to work on and take action.

The struggle with self-confidence is a struggle that all of us have to some degree. Accept that this is an area that requires constant attention. I can assure you that the people you encounter in your life who appear to be supremely confident also have moments of self-doubt. Confidence is not a genetic trait that is unchangeable, it is an attitude that can be changed.